WORLD OF WORK

BUSINESS & ADMINISTRATION

Exploring Career Pathways

Diane Lindsey Reeves

Created and produced by
Bright Futures Press, Cary, North Carolina
www.brightfuturespress.com

Published by
Cherry Lake Publishing, Ann Arbor, Michigan
www.cherrylakepublishing.com

Photo Credits: Cover, Beautyline; page 7, antoniodiaz, Fluky Fluky, David Pereiras, George Rudy, Rawpixel.com, IDin, Monkey Business Images, Rawpixel.com; page 8, antoniodiaz; page 10, Fluky Fluky; page 12, David Pereiras; page 14, George Rudy; page 16, Rawpixel.com; page 18, IDin; page 20, Monkey Business Images; Page 22, Rawpixel.com; page 24, Peshkova.

Library of Congress Cataloging-in-Publication Date

CIP data has been filed and is available at catalog.loc.gov.

Printed in the United States of America.

TABLE OF CONTENTS

HELLO WORLD OF WORK

This is you.

Right now, your job is to go to school and learn all you can.

This is the world of work.

It's where people earn a living, find purpose in their lives, and make the world a better place.

Sooner or later, you'll have to find your way from

HERE to THERE.

To get started, take all the jobs in the incredibly enormous world of work and organize them into an imaginary pile. It's a big pile, isn't it? It would be pretty tricky to find the perfect job for you among so many options.

No worries!

Some very smart career experts have made it easier to figure out. They sorted jobs and industries into groups by the types of skills and products they share. These groups are called career clusters. They provide pathways that will make it easier for you to find career options that match your interests.

- Architecture & Construction
- Arts and Communications
- Business & Administration
- Education & Training
- Finance
- Food & Natural Resources
- Government
- Health Sciences
- Hospitality & Tourism
- Human Services
- Information Technology
- Law & Public Safety
- Manufacturing
- Marketing, Sales & Service
- Science, Technology, Engineering & Mathematics (STEM)
- Transportation

Good thing you are still a kid.

You have lots of time to explore ideas and imagine yourself doing all kinds of amazing things. The **World of Work** (WoW for short) series of books will help you get started.

TAKE A HIKE!

There are 16 career pathways waiting for you to explore. The only question is: Which one should you explore first?

Is **Business and Administration** a good path for you to start exploring career ideas? There is a lot to like about this pathway. These professionals keep the companies that make our favorite products and perform important services running smoothly. They lead, support, manage, direct, and operate businesses of all types and sizes.

See if any of the following questions grab your interest.

WOULD YOU ENJOY playing Monopoly, being the boss of your favorite club or team, or starting your own business?

CAN YOU IMAGINE someday working at a big corporate headquarters, government agency, or international business center?

ARE YOU CURIOUS ABOUT what brand managers, chief executive officers, e-commerce analysts, entrepreneurs, or purchasing agents do?

If so, it's time to take a hike! Keep reading to see what kinds of opportunities you can discover along the Business and Administration pathway.

But wait!

What if you don't think you'll like this pathway?

You have two choices.

You could keep reading, to find out more than you already know. You might be surprised to learn how many amazing careers you'll find along this path.

OR

Turn to page 27 to get ideas about other WoW pathways.

DEVELOPMENT DIRECTOR

CHIEF SUSTAINABILITY OFFICER

ENTREPRENEUR

WoW Up Close

They start businesses. They make products. They provide services. They manage companies, projects, and people. These are just some of the important jobs that people who work along the Business and Administration pathway do.

SALES MANAGER

CORPORATE TRAINER

INSURANCE CLAIMS AGENT

CUSTOMER SERVICE REPRESENTATIVE

ACCOUNTANT

ACCOUNTANT

All businesses—no matter what kind or what size—have one thing in common: money. They make it, and they spend it. Someone has to keep track of where the money comes from and where it goes. That someone is an **accountant**.

Accountants are number crunchers! They use numbers to tell the story of how successful—or not—a business is.

Accuracy is the most important skill for accountants. They maintain detailed records, plan budgets, keep track of taxes, and make reports. Good accountants do more than compute numbers. A big part of the job is explaining what the numbers mean to help identify trends and plan for how to make more money and cut costs to save money. Accountants are a valuable part of the business team.

Accounting is often called the language of business. How do accountants learn this language? They usually earn a college degree in accounting or finance, and work really hard to pass a test that qualifies them as a **certified public accountant** or CPA. You can get a head start by taking lots of math classes in school. Some high schools offer finance academies where you can give accounting a test run before it's time for college.

Check It Out!

Find tips for managing a kid-sized budget at

- http://bit.ly/PBSMadMoney
- http://www.themint.org/kids
- http://bit.ly/PBSMyLifeGame

Start Now!

- Volunteer to be the "banker" the next you play a game of Monopoly with friends.
- Run for treasurer of your student government or a favorite after-school club.
- Figure out how much money it would take to buy that special something you'd really like to have and make a plan for saving up to get it.

CHIEF SUSTAINABILITY OFFICER

Sustainability is the process of doing something in a way that can be continued over time and that doesn't use up **natural resources**.

People do sustainable things when they recycle empty soda cans, reuse old furniture, and reduce the amount of water they use to brush their teeth and take a shower. That's what responsible citizens do to take care of the planet we all share.

Businesses use lots of natural resources to do what they do. Making products requires energy. Packaging products requires paper, plastic, and other materials. Getting products from the factories where they are made to the stores where people buy them requires different kinds of transportation. Many of these processes can cause pollution problems if they aren't done right. Many businesses realize that they need to be responsible citizens of their communities, too.

That's why they hire **chief sustainability officers**. These professionals make sure the business is doing all it can to recycle, reuse, and reduce the amount of natural resources used. Some of the chief sustainability officers' work involves making sure that the company follows laws and regulations about pollution and safety. A big part of their job is finding creative ways to make a difference.

Check It Out!

- http://climatekids.nasa.gov
- http://www.kidsplanet.org
- https://www3.epa.gov/recyclecity/mainmap.htm

Start Now!

- Challenge the other members of your family to see who can recycle the most. Use a chart to keep track of your progress.
- Make a poster about the three Rs—recycle, reduce, reuse—and ask your school media specialist or teacher to display it at your school.
- Use an online calculator like http://calc.zerofootprint.net to measure your carbon footprint.

CORPORATE TRAINER

Let's say you landed an after-school job at a fast-food restaurant. Yay! You'll be taking orders at the drive-through window and working the cash register. Sounds good.

Except for the fact that you have no idea how to take orders, work the drive-through communication system, or use a cash register! Good thing your new employer has a **corporate trainer** on staff to teach you all you need to know.

Everyone has to learn how to do their job well. This is true even if someone has lots of education or has been doing a certain job for a long time. Companies have specific ways of doing things. There are business systems to understand, rules to learn, procedures to follow, and technology to master. And all these things are sure to change from time to time. So, a corporate trainer tends to stay very busy!

Corporate trainers are to businesses what teachers are to schools. They teach employees—new and old—the skills and information they need to know to succeed at their jobs. This can involve leading classes, creating interactive online courses, and producing videos. Like teachers, they must know a lot about how people learn and how to teach things in ways that keep people interested.

Check It Out!

Learn how to do anything at

- http://www.wikihow.com
- http://howstuffworks.com

Start Now!

- Get practice speaking in front of others by helping teach younger kids at your place of worship or at an after-school program.
- Volunteer to teach your parent or grandparent how to play your favorite computer game.
- Use a smartphone or digital camera to record yourself demonstrating how to do something like make chocolate chip cookies or send a text message.

CUSTOMER SERVICE MANAGER

Hello, how may I help you?

And so begins another day of helping customers solve problems, find answers, and buy more products.

With these words, **customer service representatives** make a first impression (hopefully a good one!) and build a bridge between a company and its customers. They become the voice of their company.

Sometimes the job requires answering fairly simple questions: What's my account balance? When is my bill due? How do I update my online profile? Customer service representatives use computers to access this type of information and can handle many of these types of calls with no problem.

Other times, customers call with a complaint. My order got lost! I got lousy service at one of your stores! My bill is messed up! These types of callers tend to be frustrated and sometimes take out their anger on the person who answers their call. It can be a challenge, but good customer service representatives do all they can to make the customer happy before they hang up.

Other types of customer service representatives run **helpdesks** for their companies. People call or use an online message service to connect with the helpdesk, and the customer service rep **troubleshoots** their issues and gives them step-by-step solutions.

Check It Out!

Find conflict resolution tips at

- http://bit.ly/ConResA
- http://bit.ly/ConResB

Start Now!

- Try explaining your math homework to a classmate in a telephone conversation.
- Ask your parent or another trusted adult about their best and worst customer service experiences.
- Get involved in peer mediation programs at your school.

DEVELOPMENT DIRECTOR

Regular businesses do what they do to make money. They sell products and charge fees for services. But there are organizations that are in business to help people.

Think of **nonprofits** like the American Red Cross, Habitat for Humanity, and Meals on Wheels. They do what they do for free.

Even nonprofit businesses have bills, though. They have employees to pay, offices to rent, and other expenses. How do they get the money they need to do their good work?

Development directors, or fund-raisers, help them raise money from people and other businesses that care about what they do. This might involve writing grants to request money from various sources. It might involve hosting a fund-raising event like a golf tournament or a fancy dinner party.

A big part of the job is making friends with people who support the cause. It takes time and effort to keep people informed about what it happening and what the nonprofit needs. Development directors find lots of creative ways to keep in touch using social media, newsletters, and membership drives.

Check It Out!

Find out about nonprofits started by amazing kids:

- https://www.alexslemonade.org
- http://www.ladybugfoundation.ca
- http://www.fundafield.org
- http://imagination.org

Start Now!

- Volunteer to pitch in and help when your school has a fund-raiser.
- Go online to find out more about a favorite nonprofit like Make-a-Wish, St. Jude Children's Hospital, or the Humane Society.
- Talk to your parents about volunteering as a family for a local nonprofit organization.

ENTREPRENEUR

Think of a favorite product. It could be fast food, cool technology, or clothes. Pretty much anything you can think of got its start in the imagination of an **entrepreneur**. Entrepreneurs take an idea for a product or service and build a business around it.

One of the best parts of being an entrepreneur is being your own boss. The success of a new business depends on how hard—and how smart—the entrepreneur works to produce the new product and sell it to the people who need or want it.

Famous entrepreneurs you may have heard of include Bill Gates, who had an idea for an operating system that would make computers easier to use. He and a friend named Paul Allen started a company called Microsoft. Today Microsoft products are used by more than a billion people around the world. Gates now spends his time and his billions of dollars doing good things for people who need help.

Jeff Bezos is an entrepreneur who had an idea for an online store. He called it Amazon. Now, so many people around the world shop there that on its best day in 2016, it received 600 orders per second and sold more than 2 million toys, 1 million pairs of shoes, and 90,000 TVs.

Of course, not all businesses are quite that successful. But every year, many hundreds of thousands of entrepreneurs start new businesses and give it their best shot.

Check It Out!

Have fun learning about business at

- http://bizkids.com
- http://bit.ly/PBSBoss
- http://bit.ly/LemonGame

Start Now!

- Ask a local small business owner how he or she got started.
- Come up with an idea for a business you'd like to start. Give it a name and design a logo as a symbol of what it is all about.
- Use an Internet search engine to dig up information about "young entrepreneurs." A good idea and business sense often bring success for even the youngest entrepreneurs!

INSURANCE CLAIMS AGENT

In case you haven't noticed, bad things happen. One of the ways that people protect themselves is with **insurance**.

People pay money to insurance companies that agree to pay them a certain amount of money if something bad happens. There is special insurance for cars, houses, personal belongings, bad weather, health, and even death.

Say there's a windstorm that knocks a heavy tree branch down on your family's new car. The limb is so heavy that the car is squished. Having car insurance turns what would have been a very bad day into a manageable situation. The first thing your parents will do is call an **insurance claims agent**. The agent will ask them lots of questions and start a process. The agent will review your parents' coverage to figure out what their policy covers and then arrange for an insurance adjuster to estimate how much it will cost to repair or replace the car.

The claims agent will stay in touch with your parents until the situation is fixed. The job requires good people skills since they often deal with people who are experiencing tough problems. Insurance claims agents must also be very organized since they often have lots of claims at the same time.

Check It Out!

Find out more about how insurance works at

- http://playinsure.com
- http://www.tdi.texas.gov/kids/index.html

Start Now!

- Ask your parents about the different kinds of insurance your family has.
- Go online to watch "best insurance commercials" videos.

SALES MANAGER

They say a good sales manager could sell ice to an Eskimo. That means a good **sales manager** could sell anything to anyone. That kind of skill is important to businesses of all kinds and sizes.

After all, if no one buys your products or services, you won't be in business for very long!

People who work in sales are the link between a business and its customers. They must know everything there is to know about the products or services they sell. They must know everything about why a customer would need or want what they are selling. Most of all, they must know how to close the deal and get that customer to actually fork out the money to buy what they are selling.

Sales managers do exactly what the job title suggests: they manage teams of salespeople. In some cases, they manage other salespeople who work in a retail store. Their job is to train them, schedule their work hours, help out with problems, and make sure that each employee is selling, selling, selling! Other sales managers oversee teams of people who handle sales in a specific **sales territory**. This area could be a city, state, or even an entire country.

Check It Out!

Go online to visit the websites of companies that sell your favorite products. What kinds of **sales pitch** do they make to get you to buy the products?

Start Now!

- Pitch in and help out the next time your school holds a candy sale or other type of fund-raiser.
- Set up a lemonade stand and come up with creative ways to get customers to buy.
- Create a sales pitch you could use to sell a favorite product.

ACCOUNTANT • Account manager • Accounts payable manager • Accounts receivable manager • Administrative assistant • Admissions coordinator • Art director • Auditor • Banker • Billing coordinator • Biofuels manager • Bookkeeper • Brand manager • Budget analyst • Business analytics director • Business consultant • Business development director • Business teacher • Cargo agent • Channel sales director • Chief diversity officer • Chief executive officer • Chief financial officer • Chief operations officer • **CHIEF SUSTAINABILITY OFFICER** • Compliance manager • Comptroller • Computer

WoW Big List

Take a look at some of the different kinds of jobs people do in the Business and Administration pathway. **WoW!**

Some of these job titles will be familiar to you. Others will be so unfamiliar that you will scratch your head and say "huh?"

programmer • Computer technician • Construction manager • Corporate communications specialist • **CORPORATE TRAINER** • Correspondence clerk • Courier • Court clerk • Court reporter • Credit analyst • **CUSTOMER SERVICE REPRESENTATIVE** • Database administrator • Data entry clerk • **DEVELOPMENT DIRECTOR** • Dispute resolution analyst • Energy auditor • **ENTREPRENEUR** • Executive secretary • File clerk • Financial analyst • Financial examiner • Financial manager • Freight broker • General manager • Global transportation manager • Human resources manager • Human resources specialist • Information technology specialist • **INSURANCE CLAIMS AGENT** • Insurance underwriter • Labor relations manager • Law clerk • Legal secretary • Load planner • Loan processor • Logistician • Logistics coordinator • Mail carrier • Mail clerk • Management analyst • Marketing manager • Market researcher • Medical secretary • Municipal clerk • Postal worker • Print center specialist • Procurement officer • Product

Find a job title that makes you curious. Type the name of the job into your favorite Internet search engine and find out more about the people who have that job.

1. What do they do?
2. Where do they work?
3. How much training do they need to do this job?

manager • Project manager • Public information officer • Public relations coordinator • Purchasing manager • Receptionist • Registrar • Regulatory affairs manager • **SALES MANAGER** • Sales representative • Shipping and receiving clerk • Software technician • Statistician • Store manager • Sustainability specialist • Tax examiner and collector • Technical writer • Telephone operator • Treasurer • Ward clerk • Warehouse manager

TAKE YOUR PICK

	Put stars next to your 3 favorite career ideas	Put an X next to the career idea you like the least	Put a question mark next to the career idea you want to learn more about
Accountant			
Chief sustainability officer			
Corporate trainer			
Customer service representative			
Development director			
Entrepreneur			
Insurance claims agent			
Sales manager			

What do you like most about these careers?	What is it about this career that doesn't appeal to you?	What do you want to learn about this career? Where can you find answers?

Which Big Wow List ideas are you curious about?

Please do **NOT** write in this book if it doesn't belong to you. You can download a copy of this activity online at www.brightfuturespress.com/teacher-guides.

EXPLORE SOME MORE

The Business and Administration pathway is only one of 16 career pathways that hold exciting options for your future. Take a look at the other 15 to figure out where to start exploring next.

Architecture & Construction

WOULD YOU ENJOY making things with LEGOs™, building a treehouse or birdhouse, or designing the world's best skate park?

CAN YOU IMAGINE someday working at a construction site, a design firm, or a building company?

ARE YOU CURIOUS ABOUT what civil engineers, demolition technicians, heavy-equipment operators, landscape architects, or urban planners do?

Arts & Communication

WOULD YOU ENJOY drawing your own cartoons, using your smartphone to make a movie, or writing articles for the student newspaper?

CAN YOU IMAGINE someday working at a Hollywood movie studio, a publishing company, or a television news station?

ARE YOU CURIOUS ABOUT what actors, bloggers, graphic designers, museum curators, or writers do?

Education & Training

WOULD YOU ENJOY babysitting, teaching your grandparents how to use a computer, or running a summer camp for neighbor kids in your backyard?

CAN YOU IMAGINE someday working at a college counseling center, corporate training center, or school?

ARE YOU CURIOUS ABOUT what animal trainers, coaches, college professors, guidance counselors, or principals do?

Finance

WOULD YOU ENJOY earning and saving money, being the class treasurer, or playing the stock market game?

CAN YOU IMAGINE someday working at an accounting firm, bank, or Wall Street stock exchange?

ARE YOU CURIOUS ABOUT what accountants, bankers, fraud investigators, property managers, or stockbrokers do?

Food & Natural Resources

WOULD YOU ENJOY exploring nature, growing your own garden, or setting up a recycling center at your school?

CAN YOU IMAGINE someday working at a national park, raising crops in a city farm, or studying food in a laboratory?

ARE YOU CURIOUS ABOUT what landscape architects, chefs, food scientists, environmental engineers, or forest rangers do?

Government

WOULD YOU ENJOY reading about U.S. presidents, running for student council, or helping a favorite candidate win an election?

CAN YOU IMAGINE someday working at a chamber of commerce, government agency, or law firm?

ARE YOU CURIOUS about what mayors, customs agents, federal special agents, intelligence analysts, or politicians do?

Health Sciences

WOULD YOU ENJOY nursing a sick pet back to health, dissecting animals in a science lab, or helping the school coach run a sports clinic?

CAN YOU IMAGINE someday working at a dental office, hospital, or veterinary clinic?

ARE YOU CURIOUS ABOUT what art therapists, doctors, dentists, pharmacists, and veterinarians do?

Hospitality & Tourism

WOULD YOU ENJOY traveling, sightseeing, or meeting people from other countries?

CAN YOU IMAGINE someday working at a convention center, resort, or travel agency?

ARE YOU CURIOUS ABOUT what convention planners, golf pros, tour guides, resort managers, or wedding planners do?

Human Services

WOULD YOU ENJOY showing a new kid around your school, organizing a neighborhood food drive, or being a peer mediator?

CAN YOU IMAGINE someday working at an elder care center, fitness center, or mental health center?

ARE YOU CURIOUS ABOUT what elder care center directors, hairstylists, personal trainers, psychologists, or religious leaders do?

Information Technology

WOULD YOU ENJOY creating your own video game, setting up a Web site, or building your own computer?

CAN YOU IMAGINE someday working at an information technology start-up company, software design firm, or research and development laboratory?

ARE YOU CURIOUS ABOUT what artificial intelligence scientists, big data analysts, computer forensic investigators, software engineers, or video game designers do?

Law & Public Safety

WOULD YOU ENJOY working on the school safety patrol, participating in a mock court trial at school, or coming up with a fire escape plan for your home?

CAN YOU IMAGINE someday working at a cyber security company, fire station, police department, or prison?

ARE YOU CURIOUS ABOUT what animal control officers, coroners, detectives, firefighters, or park rangers do?

Manufacturing

WOULD YOU ENJOY figuring out how things are made, competing in a robot-building contest, or putting model airplanes together?

CAN YOU IMAGINE someday working at a high-tech manufacturing plant, engineering firm, or global logistics company?

ARE YOU CURIOUS ABOUT what chemical engineers, industrial designers, supply chain managers, robotics technologists, or welders do?

Marketing, Sales & Service

WOULD YOU ENJOY keeping up with the latest fashion trends, picking favorite TV commercials during Super Bowl games, or making posters for a favorite school club?

CAN YOU IMAGINE someday working at an advertising agency, corporate marketing department, or retail store?

ARE YOU CURIOUS ABOUT what creative directors, market researchers, media buyers, retail store managers, and social media consultants do?

Science, Technology, Engineering & Mathematics (STEM)

WOULD YOU ENJOY concocting experiments in a science lab, trying out the latest smartphone, or taking advanced math classes?

CAN YOU IMAGINE someday working in a science laboratory, engineering firm, or research and development center?

ARE YOU CURIOUS ABOUT what aeronautical engineers, ecologists, statisticians, oceanographers, or zoologists do?

Transportation

WOULD YOU ENJOY taking pilot or sailing lessons, watching a NASA rocket launch, or helping out in the school carpool lane?

CAN YOU IMAGINE someday working at an airport, mass transit system, or shipping port?

ARE YOU CURIOUS ABOUT what air traffic controllers, flight attendants, logistics planners, surveyors, and traffic engineers do?

MY WoW I am here.

Name

Grade

School

Who I am.

Make a word collage! Use 5 adjectives to form a picture that describes who you are.

Where I'm going.

The next career pathway I want to explore is

Some things I need to learn first to succeed.

1

2

3

To get here.

Please do **NOT** write in this book if it doesn't belong to you. You can download a copy of this activity online at www.brightfuturespress.com/teacher-guides.

GLOSSARY

accountant
person who keeps financial records for a company or business

accuracy
the quality of being correct and exact in details

certified public accountant
an accountant who has passed an official CPA test and met other requirements

chief sustainability officer
person who is in charge of a company's environmental programs

corporate trainer
person who teaches skills to employees to prepare them for a job

customer service representative
person who handles customer calls and contacts, including account inquiries, complaints, or support calls

development director
person in charge of raising funds for a nonprofit organization

entrepreneur
person who starts a new business or finds new ways to make money

helpdesks
call centers that provide customers with assistance, often with computer-related or other technical issues

insurance
an agreement in which a person pays money to a company that agrees to pay the person a certain amount of money in the event of sickness, fire, accident, or other loss

insurance claims agent
person who investigates insurance claims and recommends an effective settlement

natural resources
materials produced by the earth—such as water, forests, or minerals—that are necessary or useful to people

nonprofits
organizations that conduct business for the benefit of people instead of for the purpose of making money

sales manager
person responsible for leading and coaching a team of salespeople

sales pitch
a presentation or line of talk used to persuade someone to purchase a product or service

sales territory
the customer group or geographical area assigned to a salesperson or a sales team for sales purposes

troubleshoots
solves problems for a company or other organization

INDEX

*** Refers to the Web page sources**

About the Author

Diane Lindsey Reeves is the author of lots of children's books. She has written several original PEANUTS stories (published by Regnery Kids and Sourcebooks). She is especially curious about what people do and likes to write books that get kids thinking about all the cool things they can be when they grow up. She lives in Cary, North Carolina, and her favorite thing to do is play with her grandkids—Conrad, Evan, Reid, and Hollis Grace.